FOUR MINUTES A DAY

BY

E.C. Bernard

ILLUSTRATED BY REBECA TAYLOR DUNST

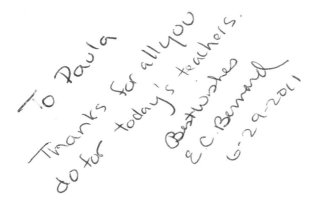

TEACHER VOICE PUBLISHING
P.O. BOX 446
VILLANOVA, PA 19085

COPYRIGHT © 2010 BY E.C. Bernard

All rights reserved, including the right of reproduction in whole or in part in any form.

For information about special discounts for bulk purchases, please contact Teacher Voice Publishing at 1-610-355-0553 or teachervoicepublishing@comcast.net.

Illustrated by Rebeca Taylor Dunst

MANUFACTURED IN
THE UNITED STATES OF AMERICA

Library of Congress Control Number: 2010926995

ISBN 978-0-9793200-7-1   0-9793200-7-0

To

all the bullied students out there who need

walking companions

and

the families of the student volunteers

for blessing the world

with their compassionate offspring

CONTENTS

Introduction 1
Entertainment Bullying 3
Jordan 13
The **"FOUR MINUTES A DAY"** Project 16
Lead Teacher 24
If You Are a Parent of a Victim 33
If You Are a Parent of a Potential Victim 37
School Administrators 43
Conclusion 50
Bibliography 52
Acknowledgments 53

INTRODUCTION

If you want to relieve the misery of a student cruelly tormented in school hallways and staircases, then this book can help you to implement your own "FOUR MINUTES A DAY" project* this week!

The goal is to relieve the victim's suffering. While we aren't able to eliminate "*entertainment bullying,*" we are able to immediately change the victim's experience in school by surrounding him with volunteers who give four minutes a day to walk with him, befriend him, and encourage him to ignore the bullies. When lovingly and thoroughly implemented, the project can improve the victim's life; while not perfect, his daily angst will be greatly reduced.

When I started such a project, two extraordinary evolutions took place.

First, a group of ordinary thirteen-year-old students in a language class evolved into a community of heroes. They and their supportive families deserve all the credit for changing the victim's despair into hope. If they can work such a miracle before they can drive a car, imagine the great things they will offer our country when they are adults!

*Four minutes represents the time secondary students have to walk in the halls changing classes, i.e. "passing time" or "change of class" time. The actual project is described on page 16.

2 INTRODUCTION

Second, many students, including bullies, allowed me to see their world through their eyes. I finally understand why they are motivated to bully and how to stop it. I evolved from a seventh-grade teacher guilty of saying, "It is a cruel age, what can we do?" to a teacher saying, "We must not abdicate our adult responsibilities to victims and bullies just because the problem is complex and difficult."

From my observations, there are two kinds of bullying, "*personal bullying*" and "*entertainment bullying.*"

3 ENTERTAINMENT BULLYING

Personal Bullying
(Bully Goes After a Specific Target)

In general, girls and some boys engage in "*personal bullying*" to improve their own social standing. They verbally attack and isolate the victim who may once have been a friend or on the fringe of their group. Their focus is to destroy their target's standing in their group. It is vicious and personal and may escalate into a physical fight.

Most experienced teachers admit they dread breaking up such a fight between two girls; I know, I'm one of them!

Girls who have engaged in this kind of bullying tell me that detentions did not deter them from engaging in this behavior. They tell me that only suspension or the threat of having to tell their parents they were going to be suspended for cruelty actually stopped them.

The good news, then, is that experienced school administrators can successfully deal with *personal bullying*. They may waste time and prolong the victim's angst as they give the bully his or her due process, i.e. warnings, detentions, and eventually threats of suspension, but they *can* make the *personal bully* stop.

4 ENTERTAINMENT BULLYING

Entertainment Bullying
(Bully Impersonally Seeks Any Responsive Target)

Both boys and girls engage in impersonal "*entertainment bullying.*" In contrast to *personal bullying*, where the behavior is targeted on a specific person, *entertainment bullying* is non-specific. It's not about the victim; it's all about the audience.

The purpose of *entertainment bullying* is to be perceived as "cool." It works when the bully succeeds in emotionally upsetting the victim, which is considered funny because it demonstrates power over someone else. Thus, the bully earns approval from the coveted audience.

While there may be many onlookers, the bully only truly cares about the response of the few students he or she is trying to impress, whom I call the "*alpha audience.*" The members of the *alpha audience* do not even have to be present, if the *entertainment bully* can then later relay the event or capture it on a cell phone.

The victims of *entertainment bullying* can be other students, substitute teachers, or any adults who respond emotionally to teasing. It is impersonal because if the target gives no response, then the bully will move on to someone else. Desired responses run the gamut from blushing, crying, screaming, swearing, fits of anger, running away, to chasing after the bully, and much more! This may explain why so many victims are those with special needs; they can't control their reactions. While *entertainment bullying* is impersonal to the bully, it is, of course, very personal to the victim.

5 ENTERTAINMENT BULLYING

From an admitted bully:

Kids who act scared out of their wits attract bullies like magnets. Bullies know they can destroy the scared ones.

In my opinion, when school administrators apply the solution to *personal bullying* (suspension/informing parents) to *entertainment bullying*, they are less successful because they rarely discover/interact with the *alpha audience*. Disciplining the bully only gives the bully something to brag about to the *alpha audience*. Their detentions are like merit badges of toughness, discussed with pride. Discipline only makes the *entertainment bully* sneakier and drives the *entertainment bullying* underground, but does not change the offensive behavior.

So what can we do?

Many students believe that the bully's parents should be told in the hopes that if parents paid more attention to their children, they would need less approval from the *alpha audience*. Some students believe that adults can't tell adolescents anything; it will just go in one ear and out the other. Other students believe that bullies need a taste of their own medicine.

6 ENTERTAINMENT BULLYING

Repeatedly, students explain that it would take the person who the bullies are trying to impress, the *alpha audience*, to decide it's not cool in order to stop the bullying. Even the *entertainment bullies* admit that they would stop if the *alpha audience* disapproves. Usually, with maturity, the *alpha audience* does move on.

Our challenge is to reach the *alpha audience* and speed up the process of moving on before the victims turn into bullies and/or self-destruct.

While "cool" kids can help the victim by surrounding him and befriending him, the key to changing bullies is to have "cool" kids also befriend the bullies.

Once I understood these dynamics, I used this information to observe and shut down a bully, Chris, in my last period class, who had been tormenting me and the class all year long.

I was perplexed by Chris's erratic behavior. I tried to identify the factors associated with the occurrences of inappropriate behavior. Finally I realized that on the days a fellow student, Ryan, had an early dismissal for sports or was absent, Chris was a great and trustworthy student.

When he was trying to impress Ryan, Chris's behavior was a nightmare. I discovered this by tracking Chris's eyes.

7 ENTERTAINMENT BULLYING

Whenever he made an inappropriate comment, his eyes darted to Ryan, who would tilt his head and raise his eyebrows in approval. Once, Ryan mouthed "good one," and I had him!

I called Ryan's mother to explain how Chris's disruptive behavior was directed at her son's approval and she agreed to discipline Ryan each time I called. She also offered to threaten Ryan that he would not be able to skateboard with Chris after school if I called again.

Ryan was horrified and incredulous that my reaction to such a little thing was equal to my reaction to Chris.

Typically, we discipline the bully, not the *alpha audience*.

Obviously, Chris's parents and my administrator gave their blessing to this behavior plan. I privately told Chris that each time he made an inappropriate comment, Ryan's mother would be against his hanging out with Ryan.

The next day the students in my period one class asked me for the spray cleaner to clean up something inappropriate. I looked at the words "I hate Mrs. Barnard" written on the top of the chair in front of Chris's desk—my only hate message since I started teaching. While the kids commented that "the loser" couldn't even spell my name right, I secretly smiled and took it as an indication that I

8 ENTERTAINMENT BULLYING

had finally reached Chris. His behavior for the rest of the year, upon redirection, was appropriate.

Teachers need to begin to ask casual questions about the alpha audience. For example, one of my 'itchy' students kept asking me when I was going to change seats. Finally I asked him who he wanted to sit with, and made a mental note. Thus, as the year progresses, if "Mr. Itchy" changes to "Mr. Disruptive" I know his alpha audience.

Another sneaky student was pretending to be using sign language but was actually making an obscene gesture while I was checking homework and being observed by an administrator. The administrator took the youngster out of the room for a discussion. A few days later, I asked who he was doing it for, as the students around him didn't know why he was out in the hall with the administrator. He admitted it was for the students across from him, and specifically named one boy. I made another mental note about his alpha audience. I didn't need it in December when the incident occurred, but filed it for later in the school year when inappropriate behavior tends to escalate.

In the beginning of the year, it is common for students to ask teachers if they know a specific student. Once the teacher acknowledges the prior relationship, i.e. the named student was a former homeroom student, or a former study hall student, the inquiring student usually explains the connection. "He's my cousin!" or "She is my dad's neighbor!" Once the school year is into its third or

9 ENTERTAINMENT BULLYING

fourth week, pay close attention when a student asks you if you have X student in one of your classes. Probe. You may be discovering an alpha audience, or something more sinister as one of my wise colleagues heard, "I was just wondering because she is bullying me on Facebook."

This book is not about the *entertainment bullies*, per se. Rather, it is about how the actions of bullies impacted one victim and what we did to help him.

People who have been told this story and the anecdotal research that I share on *entertainment bullying* frequently comment, "But you are just a language teacher, how did you come up with this?"

I have no degree in psychology, no training in special education or counseling, and no interest in performing empirical research. But I do have an open heart and communicate to my students my belief in their goodness and potential, even if they are the ones who bully. Hence, the *entertainment bullies* have shared their truth with me.

I am sharing it with you because every school year vulnerable students leave the cocoon of their small elementary school classroom and travel unmonitored staircases and hallways while switching classes for the first time in middle school, junior high, or high school.

In many districts, it is the first time that children from homogenous elementary schools learn to co-exist with students from different socio-economic backgrounds.

10 ENTERTAINMENT BULLYING

As students jockey for position in the new social hierarchy, they try to be funny and impress their new *alpha audience* by finding easy victims to bully. With ubiquitous text messaging, a gang of students can easily converge and watch the entertainment bullies. Sometimes students take turns tormenting a victim and keeping score of what they had done to him via texts and face-to-face conversations.

When the *entertainment bullying* persists, there are two likely outcomes:

1. The victim may resort to retaliatory tactics that turn him or her into a bully that other students will be reluctant to help.

2. The victim may sink into a depression and/or self-destruct.

This annual ritual is so unnecessary and dangerous.

By sharing the information about good-hearted adolescents rising to the challenge of " **FOUR MINUTES A DAY**", the hope is that when, for any reason, a child becomes *the* persistent target for bullies, the adults in the school will creatively come up with a similar project to keep that child from feeling isolated.

11 ENTERTAINMENT BULLYING

Isolation is unhealthy.

When students like our victim arrive in September, they are sweet children who hunger to learn, and within their classes, re-establish the community experienced in elementary school. But isolated and taunted during passing time, they began to retaliate with the meanness that others direct at them.

I have since learned of another boy who was taunted and began to steal from the other students to retaliate. He now has a police record. He is fortunate; some self-destruct.

My fear is that when students transition from elementary schools to a Middle School or a Junior High where they must switch classes, there is only a small window of opportunity to intervene before the unprotected victims become equally and unnecessarily cruel.

I am ashamed to confess that before my project, while I was aware that we had to be vigilant in the halls, I reasoned this was the administrators' problem to resolve by disciplining the bullies.

12 ENTERTAINMENT BULLYING

In the beginning of the year, we teachers vaguely told other students to let us know of the problems they observed in the halls, but we didn't give them the concrete directive of assigning them four minutes a day. The vagueness made it everyone's responsibility and thus no one's responsibility, and the entertainment bullies found nooks and blind spots in the building to torment students like "Jordan."

JORDAN

What kind of victim benefits from a "FOUR MINUTES A DAY" project? Usually the victim is someone like "Jordan." (Jordan is used to personalize the word "victim" and because Jordan can be either a boy or a girl. I will refer to Jordan as a 'he' for the purpose of continuity.) Jordan is a composite of the kind of student who is emotionally safe in the classroom with teachers and classmates, but who generally walks alone between classes and is the target for entertainment bullies. He may be very intelligent, quite musical, exceptionally punctual, and makes unusual, almost poetic observations that are quite accurate.

Conversations with Jordan are atypical for someone his age. He often speaks formally, like a little professor, yet eschews dressing for style and prefers to dress for comfort, like an elementary school student.

Jordan tends to obsess on a few specific subjects and is oblivious to most social cues. Paradoxically, he can be very sensitive and intensely emotional. Entertainment bullies delight in using these obsessions to create an uncontrollable emotional reaction. It makes them feel powerful, especially if the victims are academically high achievers.

When Jordan reacts to both perceived and actual teasing, he can quickly have a meltdown. It may take a while for Jordan to recover, and it may take a while for other students to accustom themselves to these meltdowns, but most students in public middle school have been raised with inclusion in the classroom. They know to enjoy the good moments and give space during meltdowns.

Classmates with strong teachers create a positive and safe environment in the classroom. The problems occur outside the classroom, when Jordan is usually alone. His classmates should not be blamed for his walking alone. Generally Jordan is obsessed with getting to class on time and can almost knock down other students in his pursuit to avoid a detention for tardiness.

Jordan is focused on getting to class on time, but is also anxious navigating the hallways and stair cases and gym changing rooms as the entertainment bullies know all the right places to make remarks out of earshot of teachers and hall aides. Once the teasing, either real or imagined begins, Jordan's level of anxiety rises and he is unable to ignore the remarks, in spite of numerous adults instructing him to do so. This is the point where he begins to retaliate and to an adult approaching the scene, it appears that Jordan is the problem as the other students are in control of themselves and he clearly is not.

To further clarify the imagined teasing, Jordan may be accustomed to some students laughing at him at a particular location at a particular time of day. Therefore, even if that group isn't there, or it is a different time of day, Jordan may perceive that the different group,

15 JORDAN

laughing about something else and even unaware of his presence, is laughing at him. His reaction is the same to this imagined teasing as it is to real teasing: he defends himself and addresses the unaware group. They are startled and they perceive a "crazy" person lashing out at them for no reason and, thus, they feel unjustifiably assaulted.

The disciplinarians in the building want to protect Jordan from the bullies, but also receive reports of him being the perpetrator, and so Jordan loses some of his automatic 'victim' status.

Thus, a sweet student entering a new Middle School or Junior High can turn into an anxious and angry person with a constant chip on the shoulder and no friends.

THE SOLUTION IS TO START

A "FOUR MINUTES A DAY" PROJECT.

---

16 A "FOUR MINUTE A DAY" PROJECT

THE "FOUR MINUTES A DAY" PROJECT

In this project, different groups of two or three volunteers engage Jordan in conversation walking between classes and after school to Jordan's locker.

The students are asked to keep the organized project a class secret. The entertainment bullies don't quite know what is happening, but become aware that it is very hard to get their target alone.

The beauty of this project and the key to its success is that each group of students only takes one passing time slot. The entertainment bullies are thwarted from provoking a reaction from Jordan because he is busy talking with his walking companions. Since it is always a different group of students, it doesn't appear to be organized.

The teacher creates a master schedule to help the volunteers and Jordan to keep track of their commitments, which should include pictures of each volunteer. Extra copies should be sent to Jordan's family, because practicing social skills in real time with other students can help Jordan.

17 A "FOUR MINUTE A DAY" PROJECT

While the students do their part, Jordan's family should help by using the master schedule to encourage Jordan to:

- ♥ learn all of the volunteers' names
- ♥ learn one fact about each student each week
- ♥ ask each group, "What did you do this weekend?"

The family may be pleasantly surprised with the results of their efforts!

Within two months of starting such a project one mother wrote:

I had to share with you a really amazing observation I had last night following the band concert. Typically after those performances my son is ready to get out the door as fast as he can.

Last night he asked me to wait a bit while he went over to say hi to a few friends (right there was my first pleasant surprise). As I watched him move through the crowd, I saw him engaged with fellow classmates in high-fives and hand shakes, as he was complimenting them on the good job they did on the concert.

This has never happened before following any school event. It was amazing to see. He was smiling and laughing and kids

18 A "FOUR MINUTE A DAY" PROJECT

were not turning away from him or rolling their eyes as they would usually do (I have had some pretty painful moments watching kid's reactions to him), and he even brought a few over to introduce them to me.

It was truly the first time I ever experienced my son being spontaneously and appropriately social, and happy to be a part of the scene. What a gift that was!

The volunteers are encouraged to let Jordan talk about his two main interests, usually scenes from TV and video games.

Typically, Jordan is very anxious to have friends. So, even if there is an incidence with bullies saying something, Jordan will usually respond to the volunteers hustling him along keeping him engaged, as he does savor his friends' attention and he is focused on his interests. Therefore, his reaction is quite diminished in comparison to when he walks alone. **Talking to friends was described as the only switch that will help Jordan to tune out the annoying mosquito buzzing of cruel remarks.**

In my opinion, Jordan is neurologically wired to be who he is destined to be. This project doesn't change that wiring, but it does significantly lower his anxiety during passing time and gives him the opportunity to practice social skills. Thus, Jordan may increase his ability to cope and expand his emotional intelligence.

19 A "FOUR MINUTE A DAY" PROJECT

For example, if there is an incident where another student bumps into Jordan, he may interpret the act as intentional while the companions interpret the act as accidental. While the volunteers may not be able to sway Jordan from his interpretation, accompanied by others, the incident may not lead to a meltdown as it probably would have if Jordan had been alone. Even Jordan realizing, *in the moment*, that someone else might interpret the incident differently will be a sign of progress for him.

Speaking of meltdowns, the project will not eliminate meltdowns. Unexpected changes in the schedule, substitute teachers, assemblies, losing a competitive review game in class or in gym, a sad story about an animal, fire drills, etc. could all contribute to a meltdown.

However, the project will expand the community of people who 'get' the Jordans of the world and widen the circle of peers who can see past his differences and relate to him.

The project will enrich the lives of the volunteers. Teachers will be amazed at the cross section of students who will volunteer, and it may be the only opportunity for the student dressed in black with bright green hair to walk with a cheerleader and a student council member during their assigned slot.

20 A "FOUR MINUTE A DAY" PROJECT

For this peer-support project, it is important for the lead teacher to be given the time to create a sense of community. The lead teacher should be relieved of homeroom duty and of any other non-teaching duty.

If the teacher sees the volunteers during the course of the day, then constant daily interactions and e-mail will suffice. From the beginning, the volunteers should be sent e-mails of encouragement every ten days or so. In return, volunteers can send e-mails of their experiences, or else write in a class journal.

If the lead teacher doesn't see all of the students in class, then it would be helpful to meet every Monday during homeroom. During this time, students should hand in a sheet about problems and observations. The lead teacher then meets with the students during 'duty' time to problem solve.

The volunteers' commitment may help to smooth out their own rough waters of adolescence. Volunteers may be typical junior high adolescents, trying out some undesirable behaviors that need corrections, yet they also experience a sense of pride, community, and accomplishment for their "FOUR MINUTES A DAY" commitment. One student, who was disciplined for being

21 A "FOUR MINUTE A DAY" PROJECT

a bully in seventh grade, became a volunteer in eighth grade after apologizing and asking to make amends.

One volunteer wrote about her experience:

I realized the little things in life one may do, can make a big difference in someone else's life.

(Previously) I didn't know him very well, But, I came to a conclusion through out the school year that he's a really nice, friendly, normal human being. One I could call as a friend.

The volunteers' parents should be contacted and praised for specific things their children say or do. Parents will encourage their children and help them to process their experiences. Even if one volunteer is being disciplined for other lapses in judgment, he or she will be complimented for his or her actions with the "FOUR MINUTES A DAY" project.

The parents of one volunteer expressed:

We think that perhaps you've given these children a license to care and that is a very cool thing. We are all responsible for each other and the sooner we learn that the better off the world will be.

The mother from page 12 also wrote:

My son has been the target of constant teasing starting from the first day of 7th grade. I can't even tell you how much stress and strain the teasing has placed on our family. We were really at a breaking point emotionally. The *"FOUR MINUTES A DAY"* project has literally changed his whole perception of school now and has changed our lives at home. He no longer walks in the door from school crying and hating school. He is actually happy.

A different student observed at the end of the year:

At the beginning of the year I saw (him) being bullied but now I see him as popular and cool...he has great educational skills. He could be very successful in his life and I think he will be able to do that.

Finally, in one victim's own words:

*Before this alliance was formed, I thought I would have lost hope. Kids were constantly teasing me ... and I was even considering missing school! Once you stepped in with this project, those problems were vanquished and done with. I feel safer now that I walk with students in the halls. Plus, I am even starting to make new friends. Thanks a ton for starting the **"FOUR MINUTES A DAY"** Project.*

23 A "FOUR MINUTE A DAY" PROJECT

Since the "FOUR MINUTES A DAY" project helped 'our' Jordan, it might help others. It takes a willing teacher with flexible colleagues, administrative support vis-à-vis ample time for the lead teacher to administer the project, and weekly snacks for volunteers willing to donate four minutes a day. If you want to set up a project for someone you know:

Parents of Potential Victims go to pages 36 - 41

  Parents of Victims go to pages 33 – 35

    Administrators go to pages 42 – 49

      Teachers go to pages 24 – 32

LEAD TEACHER

If you are the lead teacher, this is what you need to know.

Consult with Jordan about his schedule and figure out where help is needed. Parents and administrators thought that help was needed all day, but it turned out there were parts that were fine as the teachers were in the halls and the rooms were close.

You will need to assign more students to the portions that involve walking through the cafeteria or up several flights of stairs. Jordan may be fine with one person if it were a straight shot from one room on the second floor to another room on the second floor, but may need extra help from gym, through the cafeteria, to the third floor. Even if he is fine with one person, assign two as there are many reasons why one student may not be available, i.e. staying behind to finish a test, called down to guidance, out for a dental appointment, field trip, illness, choir practice, etc. This will ensure that Jordan is not alone.

Even if Jordan's locker is located along a short distance route, it is a magnet for bullies and Jordan should be accompanied at his locker.

You might be looking at Jordan's schedule on paper but it probably doesn't reveal when he is truly in study hall, because he may have many 'pull-outs' for speech therapy, meeting with his guidance counselor, and other services.

25 LEAD TEACHER

You will have to ask specifically each day if he is truly in that study hall.

You need to think about the teachers on the schedule. Two girls were frustrated because the new social studies teacher spent a lot of time doing projects in the library and it was necessary to create a way to inform them so that they went to the right place.

Lunch time poses all kinds of problems.

In many secondary schools, two-thirds of the teachers are teaching and one third is monitoring study halls opposite lunch. Consequently, as students switch from lunch to study hall, there aren't as many adults in the halls as they are teaching full periods. Students are instructed to go to their lockers on their way to lunch and bullies know exactly where to find their targets with little adult supervision in the halls. **Make sure you include extra escorts to and from lunch.**

As for lunch itself, some schools have assigned seating and some have open seating with a lot of unstructured movement between multiple lunch rooms. Jordan may have one good friend from elementary school and everything possible should be done to assign them to the same lunch period. If told that it is impossible to switch around the schedule mid-year to accommodate a lunch change, it could be pointed out that it will save the administration countless hours of resolving future discipline issues as many problems occur during lunch.

26 LEAD TEACHER

But perhaps there is no candidate to be his lunch buddy.

From an adult perspective, you may think it best to ask the volunteers to rotate inviting him to their lunch table. I hesitate to do so because students are so vulnerable at this age with their own lunch table status. They may be willing to quietly give four minutes a day but are not comfortable letting everyone know that they are doing this. If Jordan shows up at their table every Tuesday, they would be forced to reveal to others what they do, and I sense it would create resentment and make the project backfire. For more suggestions about lunch, see the section for school administrators, number 6.

Now that you have a good idea about how many students you will need to accompany Jordan, it is time to compose your talk to potential volunteers. If you teach Jordan, start with that class. Ask Jordan if he wants to be in the room when the request is made; otherwise make arrangements for him to leave the last ten minutes of class and be somewhere else.

The lead teacher needs to come up with the right words to formulate the request. Consider:

♥ If there is a famous person or local hero that students admire? Tell them that you will be sending one another emails or writing in the class journal about the experience and will send a version of it to the hero.

27 LEAD TEACHER

♥ If there is a homogenous religion to draw upon, incorporate those values into the project. Some walkers are encouraged by their families to ask "What would Jesus do?" and some walkers are encouraged to do little 'mitzvahs' for others.

♥ Remind students of the periods in time when ordinary people have done the right thing, i.e. helping to abolish slavery, helping women to obtain the right to vote, helping the Jews during the Holocaust, etc. Remind them that this is their chance to do the right thing.

♥ Review and condense President Obama's inaugural speech, calling on American to give service, if that will appeal to your students.

♥ Discuss any service obligations that your school may have for graduation and discuss which is more meaningful; to do it for a couple of weeks for strangers or to do it for four minutes a day for a classmate?

♥ Remind them of the Spanish proverb "In our lives, we have two or three opportunities to be a hero, but almost every day, we have the opportunity not to be a coward."

♥ Conclude with the idea that they may not get back from the student what they get back from other students but that in your heart you believe they would be better off for the experience. Remind them that this is class secret and they are not to discuss this outside the room except at home with their families.

28   LEAD TEACHER

If passing time, i.e. the time allotted to students to change classes, is four minutes, then asks the other students if they would be willing to specifically donate four minutes a day, and just four minutes a day, to help.

Have a few clipboards with sign - up sheets and tell them that soon you will be in touch with their assigned four minute slot. It is better to assign slots apart from the students because you don't want it to be about little cliques taking turns. The goal is to give an inspiring presentation, create a frenzy of signing up, and then students move on, as class is over. Secure the volunteers schedules and make up your master schedule. Ask volunteers to share their family contact info.

Or, hand out copies of their schedules and ask them to pass them in with their family contact info, i.e., names, phone numbers and e-mail addresses of their parents, if they are interested in helping. Ask them to circle the time slot that would work for them if they share other classes with Jordan. If they don't know Jordan's schedule because they don't share any other classes together, assure them that you will figure it out. Collect all the sheets, that way no one can tell who is willing and who isn't.

If there are some holes in the schedule, request the class rosters for Jordan's classes. You might spot other students to include. Consult with the Jordan's teachers and ask for their input. Consider having the students leave some trouble spots a minute earlier.

29 LEAD TEACHER

As you make up the schedule, use a digital camera to insert pictures. Share it with Jordan's family so that they take the steps mentioned on page 17 and so that they can encourage Jordan to wait for the volunteers, and not rush out of the room.

Give one to all of the volunteers so that they know who else is helping. Do not put Jordan's name or picture on it in case one becomes misplaced.

Once the schedule is set, inform the teachers of the volunteers about the project. Ask them to help the volunteers to remember until it becomes a habit. Request flexibility if the volunteer leaves two minutes early or arrives two minutes late.

Use the business cards that come ten to a sheet to make passes with the students' pictures and the time and classes that are impacted. Probably your office has a laminator for business cards for replacement bus passes. Laminate it for the volunteers to use as a reminder and as a pass if there is a substitute. On the back of the card, list the lead teacher's room extension, a back-up teacher extension, and the appropriate principal's extension. Tell the students if there is a bad problem in the hall, to go into the closest room, show the card, and ask the teacher to call the numbers on the back for help.

30 LEAD TEACHER

E.C. Bernard May leave 2 minutes early from room 234 period 4 may be 2 minutes late to room 105 T Th to room 219 MWF	

Train yourself and the students to be aware of changes in the school day for assemblies, late arrivals because of weather, early dismissals, etc. These small changes create havoc and you will need to remind the students of the alternative plan.

With the schedule complete, it is time to build a sense of community. If you don't see the volunteers in class, arrange to meet every Monday during homeroom. Provide a snack and have them submit the weekly observation form. Always have extra copies easily available in your room or the guidance office or on the share drive. On the form ask them to advise you of any problems or observations they want to share. If they are out Monday, they can e-mail it to you. If there is a crisis, encourage them to find you immediately.

If you see the students in class, set up a group e-mail list to facilitate contact and have an interesting small notebook with lined paper for the students who prefer to write.

31 LEAD TEACHER

I didn't provide a notebook at first, because I assumed this generation uses the computer so much, but that was my stereotype and not necessarily true. Many prefer to write in the book.

Send out group e-mails to the volunteers and their parents twice a month about what you have observed and what others are saying about them. Praise them by mentioning specific observations. (Jordan is not on this mailing list.)

Frequently contact the parents of the volunteers, preferably by phone. Praise their child. Encourage a dialogue with the parents, something harder to do in e-mail. You may be surprised by what you learn about what is happening in the halls as students share with their parents without a filter.

Keep the lines of communication open with the victim's parents. Keep your eye on the goal of making things better, don't be discouraged by setbacks if the general trend is an improvement and the victim is happier most days.

32   LEAD TEACHER

Include all stakeholders, administrators, guidance counselors, special educators, if applicable, in your project. If you work in a large building, maybe give two minute monthly updates at faculty meetings and encourage all to be aware of situation.

As other teachers start creating their own projects, I hope they will contact me and I will post their news and questions on a blog. So please contact me:
>   my e-mail: **e.c.bernard@comcast.net**
>   (please note periods)
>
>   my website: **www.ecbernard.org**

If a parent asks you to open your heart and schedule to helping their child, do it.

If you know a child is being bullied all day long, do it.

You will feel a depth of emotion for your volunteers and victim that will enrich your life.

Remember *The Starfish Story* by Loren Eisley[2] about the boy throwing starfish back into the ocean even though the adult warned him it didn't matter, he couldn't help them all? His reply was that it would matter to the one he helped.

33 PARENT OF A VICTIM

IF YOU ARE THE PARENT OF A VICTIM

If you are reading this, I trust that you have gone to your school guidance counselor, vice principal, principal and they are aware of the situation and are disciplining those bullies they have caught, but the situation is persisting.

Right now you are tempted to take this book and request that a similar project be instituted for your own child.

First, get your facts straight with documentation. While Jordan may be upset at all the mean kids bothering him all day long, his parents need to listen and decipher that it may actually be the halls and lunch time that are really the problem. Then, as you delve further through the schedule, there may actually be a few passing times that aren't problems at all. Go through your child's schedule and decipher the actual trouble spots. Be prepared to ask for help for specific segments.

Second, you will have to decide if you should directly ask a teacher, who would have to secure administrative approval, or if you should ask the school administrator, who would have to find a teacher to lead it.

Once you decide, compose a letter outlining the pain your child is experiencing and how it impacts the family. Express your fear that your child's isolation may lead to major problems. Include this book and ask that a teacher set up a project for the documented trouble spots similar

34 PARENT OF A VICTIM

to Jordan's project, to ensure your child's academic success.

Whichever compassionate teacher is picked, give them:

my e-mail: e.c.bernard@comcast.net (note periods)

my website: www.ecbernard.org

I *will* respond and they will find information for sharing the process with me and other teachers via a blog on my website.

But your part doesn't end there. If your child is a target for bullying, you must have the courage to examine your child's part in the equation. Please think about your child's bullying. Is he/she a victim of *personal bullying* or *entertainment bullying?*

If the former, encourage your child to make new friends, join new clubs, and participate in new activities.

If the latter, *entertainment bullies* are attracted to students who give a desired emotional reaction and are attracted to students who act afraid. This is an undoubtedly difficult question to answer, but why do you think they are attracted to your child? If you are resisting answering this question, and just want the school to focus on the bullies, then your denial will prevent you from truly helping your child, and your child deserves to be helped.

35 PARENT OF A VICTIM

Let me share my favorite Brazilian legend about the "Pai Coruja."

This "father owl" was enamored with his three new babies. He begged the predator, the hawk, to leave his babies alone. The hawk agreed and asked for a description so that he wouldn't eat this owl's babies. The *pai coruja* described them as beautiful, strong, smart, and bright-eyed. A few days later, the babies were missing and a sparrow told the *pai coruja* that the hawk had eaten them! When the *pai coruja* confronted the hawk, he exclaimed, "I didn't know they were yours because they were so ugly, weak, and stupid!"

I love this legend because it warns parents that only by abandoning their illusions about their children can they truly protect them.

So to evaluate, and perhaps change your child, will not be easy. Our middle class American culture today is such that parents react so negatively to unflattering information about their child that they will want to sue you if you are not family and shun you if you are.

Hence, parents may be isolated from valuable information from teachers and family members. My sense is that if you truly want to help your child, the victim of bullying, you may have to go to a good counselor to get to the heart of the matter.

36 PARENT OF A VICTIM

Being able to tell the school administrators, "We know that our child needs to X and we will be working on this," will go a long way in encouraging them to work with you and to set up this project.

37 POTENTIAL VICTIM

IF YOU ARE A PARENT OF A POTENTIAL VICTIM ENTERING A NEW BUILDING

If your child has a history of being a victim, and is entering a new building, you are probably tempted to call the guidance counselor with your concerns.

Instead, I suggest that you have the guidance counselor, previous classroom teacher, or principal of the elementary school contact the guidance counselor at the new school and explain the previous history. The elementary school official can request that:

1. X friend be put on the same team so that the student has at least one friend in some of the same classes.

2. Arrangements be made for at least one friend as a lunch companion.

3. Thoughtful consideration be given to the student's locker location.

4. Any previously identified bullies not be in the same class as your student. (One year a student's family was bringing another student to court over a sexual harassment issue. They never told anyone at the school and somehow these two were enrolled in five of the same class every day!)

Unfortunately, if the parent makes this request, it may come across as a manipulative, anxious parent and the guidance counselors know if they arrange it for one parent, it will open the floodgates. However, if a school administrator, guidance counselor, or classroom teacher calls because of the history, and uses the magical phrase "to ensure this student's academic success" there is a stronger likelihood of getting results.

But your part doesn't end there. If your child was a target for bullying, **you must have the courage to examine your child's part in the equation.** Does your child act afraid? Does your child overreact to real and/or imagined slights? Is your child so literal that he or she misses many social cues?   If you are unsure about this, please see pages 34 and 35.

In the beginning, our Jordan did act afraid, attracting the bullies. Then, he reacted to their teasing, unwittingly inviting their prolonged interest in him. While Jordan's parents and the school worked with him on his reactions, the key to changing his being afraid was to remove his isolation, with a safety net of companions.

You might be tempted to wait and see what the new school year brings and if there is a problem, hope that a "**FOUR MINUTES A DAY**" project solves it. I suggest you be more proactive.

You should take advantage of the time before entering the new school to figure out why your child has been targeted. In addition to seeing a counselor, there are some things you can do to help your child enter the new building. Up to now, you have encouraged your child to be his or her

39 POTENTIAL VICTIM

own unique person. However, for the next few years, the key to not being teased will be to blend in and not stand out. How do you do this?

Instill confidence in your child's ability to find new rooms. If the school has a map of the building layout, highlight your child's new classrooms and if possible go over the sequence so that your child can act with confidence. Also highlight the guidance office and nurse's office for adult support, bathrooms and locker. Figure out which classes are close to one another and use passing time between those two classes to use the bathroom.

I'm unsure how to explain this next idea, but you need the inside scoop of the building to help your child. For example, each building has certain things that automatically confer "geek" status on you, similar to painting a target on your back with a sign saying "bullies look here."

In our building, it's:

1. showing up with a book bag with wheels on it (Sorry, please spare me the excuses about the child's back, he or she just needs to learn how to use his or her locker. This is a safety issue, students with bags with wheels stop at the top of the stairs to pick up the bag and everyone behind them stumbles into them.)

2. trying to use one big binder for all eight classes.

3. juvenile lunchboxes instead of lunch bags.

40 POTENTIAL VICTIM

4. eyeglass frames from third grade that need to be updated.

5. boys wearing pants they have clearly outgrown and are two inches above their ankles. (What does your son need to wear to fit in? jeans? Time to retire the comfy sweats?)

6. girls wearing juvenile cutesy shirts.

7. girls wearing hair accessories that no one else in the building wears.

8. stained shirts.

9. socks – one year it's only wear white, the following year, never wear white – I can't keep up but some years it's important.

10. unwashed hair/poor grooming (The last week of summer before entering the new building, you need to train your adolescent to take a daily morning or evening shower.)

11. hairstyles that make it hard to figure out the student's gender.

How do you figure this out?

Network to find a reliable student already in the new building. It could be a neighbor, a volunteer at the local park, or older brother or sister of a classmate. Ask them to complete this sentence, "You know on day one that the

41 POTENTIAL VICTIM

new kid is a geek if ...." If you can't find anyone, just watch students getting off the bus near your house, or gather your courage and contact the new school's PTO and offer to volunteer and ask for help.

Courageously examine your own reaction to being told that something draws unwanted attention.

One boy established little eye contact, walked one step ahead of his walking companions with his shoulders hunched over as if he were 'charging' forward, and had 'floppy' arm movements. At first, his parents were doubtful that they should try to change his gait, his way of moving, *his way of being*. However, this is what attracted the attention of the bullies. His parents enrolled him in 'play therapy' outside of school and told him that he only had to attend five times and then they would re-evaluate its value. There, he learned to strengthen his inner core. When he chooses, he can now concentrate and walk and move in such a way that blends in with the crowd. The parents are now believers.

Another girl drew unwanted attention to herself because of her hair bows from a different decade. Since her teacher's own son was friends with the girl's brother, the teacher thought she could help the girl be less of a target for bullies by talking to the girl's mom, someone she knew from their sons' soccer games. When the teacher mentioned that it might help to blend in better by ditching the bows in favor of a more current hairstyle, the parent

42 POTENTIAL VICTIM

exploded on her acquaintance. The mom explained she personally loved the little girl look it gave her daughter and that everyone should just tolerate this difference.

If you have a similar reaction to something on the list on the previous pages, **you need to examine the cost to your child for your belief system.** Once your child is out of middle school or junior high, he or she can return to being unique.

Finally, from what I have observed and read, a student truly needs just one good friend to survive.

Do everything you can to help your child to nurture that friendship. Continue to provide your child with opportunities to practice developing friends. Many of our less social students volunteer at the school store or school library. Help your child to find one activity or club to join at the beginning of the year before the new social hierarchy is set in stone.

43 SCHOOL ADMINISTRATORS

IF YOU ARE A SCHOOL ADMINISTRATOR

If you are not satisfied with the level of bullying in your school, consider the following seven suggestions.

1. Train your staff to distinguish between *personal bullying* and *entertainment bullying* and resist the temptation to treat them as being the same. Once the disciplinarian in your building has identified the entertainment bully, gather information from your teachers, hall aides, lunch aides, librarians, coaches, students, parents and secretaries as to the identity of the bully's *alpha audience*. Once you have the connection, make the link between bullying and separating the bully from the *alpha audience*. Bring in both sets of parents. Be creative.

2. If a teacher is going to start a "FOUR MINUTES A DAY" project, show your support by assigning someone else to take over his or her duty period and homeroom duty.

Students drop by during homeroom for many reasons:

- ♥ they have an early dismissal for a doctor's appointment.

- ♥ they have a field trip or an all-day chorus rehearsal.

- ♥ they want the teacher to know that another volunteer is absent and someone needs to cover that slot.

The duty time is needed to compensate for the initial upfront work and to manage the project without creating teacher burnout. When I first put together the volunteer schedule, deciphered Jordan's true schedule with all of its "pull-outs" not on paper, and made passes for volunteers and informed the teachers of the volunteers of what was going on, it took over ten hours of one of my weekends. Being relieved of a duty would begin to compensate for that.

The duty period needs to be used to compose encouraging bi-monthly e-mails of encouragement, arrange coverages for unavailable students and students who go home sick, contact parents and other teachers.

The teacher/coordinator always needs time to trouble-shoot daily problems. Even teenagers with the best intentions to help can easily be distracted and need "in-the-moment" prompts that only classroom teachers can provide. Guidance counselors are usually too removed from the classrooms to be able to provide in-the-moment prompts.

3. Better yet, create a duty into the schedule. Call it a "tutorial," if necessary, but don't assign any students. Rather, as soon as reports of bullying crop up, the teacher assigned to this duty will start working on identifying the alpha audience, deciphering the timing and location of the bullying and connecting the student with other students to cover that vulnerable part of the schedule.

4. How do you go about selecting a teacher? The classroom teacher who leads this project should be the kind of teacher who believes in the good of every student and can appeal to students' higher moral level by inviting them to participate, not someone who will assign students a job.

The teacher needs to be flexible and not hold it against the students when they forget or make mistakes. While the teacher acknowledges how hard it can be, he or she also encourages the students and their parents by praising them privately and continuing to affirm his or her belief in them. Obviously the teacher should volunteer to do this; it most likely won't be successful if it is an unwanted assigned duty.

During the second year of this project, a special education teacher wanted to take this on as I no longer had the students in class. She admitted that special education teachers don't know the students in the main-streamed classes who would be willing to help, so it needs to be a joint effort of a classroom teacher and a special education teacher; the special ed teachers just don't have the contacts. She holds once a week breakfasts for the students to connect with them. On the days she is absent, the students come to me with glitches.

5. Fight the temptation to publicize this project. The students walking with our Jordan told their close friends but it was never widely known. I think that helped them not to become targets themselves. Since each student just donated four minutes a day, it didn't seem like Jordan had "a wrap-around" hall aide. He was just always surrounded by different students. The bullies didn't find out that the other students were organized until the Awards Ceremony at the end of the year.

Fortunately, on the day I made my pitch to the class for volunteers, one particular student was absent. This student tends to slink around the building trading tidbits of information, inciting others, and creating drama.

Upon his return, no one bothered to tell him about the project. For whatever reason, the students spoke in code around him, and when they would talk to me about their experience, or ask to write in the book, they did it outside his earshot. However, he did unwittingly participate as he happened to walk with the students who also happened to be walking with our Jordan.

On the day our Jordan's parents brought in snacks, as a thank-you gesture to the class, he exclaimed "I knew something was going on – what was it?" I now believe that the students were protecting one another's privacy, and that it is important to keep this low-key.

6. In the summer, when schedules are sent home to students entering a new building, the biggest anxiety is

SCHOOL ADMINISTRATORS

finding a friendly face with the same lunch period. Many parents have approached me during the tour day while I was setting up my room to see if I could find a list of students eating lunch during the same time their child eats lunch. They just wanted to reassure their child that they would know someone, even if their numerous calls to other parents have yielded nothing. Parents know that teachers will create a community in their classes or teams, but that lunch is very unstructured.

Administrators know that a lot of their time is devoted to settling lunch time problems. Consider building solutions into the schedule as the master schedule is created. For example, before starting to schedule, have the guidance counselors actively solicit the elementary school principals about students who are loners or tend to be bullied. If the child has one friend, schedule them together.

In one building, a teacher from each team gives up lunch on the first day to sweep the cafeteria looking for lone eaters. The student names are noted and the student is asked, "Are any of your friends now in study hall? Who?" Flipping the lunch on day two and giving all students an eating companion goes a long way in eliminating future problems.

Actively create alternatives to a student sitting alone during lunch. What rooms are near the cafeteria? In one school, the art teacher's duty wasn't a study hall, per se, rather his room was open and the lone eaters were encouraged to keep the teacher company. One year, students mocked and threw trash at one particular introvert, so he started eating in the art room. The following year, with a different schedule, he continued to eat while the teacher held class.

Consider creating a lunch bunch type group for kids like Jordan. Perhaps a club or group for whatever interest they have (chess club, computers, etc.) and those kids could band together or eat in a special room together. Create an empty study hall for a teacher near the cafeteria who would be willing to sponsor such a lunch time activity.

Sometimes it is easier just to have an aide assigned to Jordan, so he can eat in a small room, but that doesn't teach him better social skills or coping skills. Another solution is to let Jordan eat quickly and then go to the library to read.

7. Train the 'cool' kids who are volunteers to approach the alpha audience and convince them that bullying isn't cool. Don't do it over the announcements or with motivational speakers or any other formal setting. It needs to be select, individualized, informal, and personal.

In my own class, no one picked on 'our' Jordan. But on the days I had a substitute, one boy would set our Jordan up by making sexual innuendos that he didn't understand in an attempt to impress two specific girls in the class. I believe he did it because Jordan was so obviously academically talented and this boy was repeating seventh

49 SCHOOL ADMINISTRATORS

grade and in danger of repeating again. He made himself look "street smart" at Jordan's expense, and that he was much cleverer than the "smart kid" in the class.

Others in the class would tell me about this upon my return. Once the two girls started to walk with Jordan, they became very protective of him. Thereafter, when a substitute took over the class for me, this boy no longer made his attempts to look clever as his *alpha audience* would not put up with his antics. I once asked the two girls why they thought it was funny when he did this and they told me, "We used to laugh along with him because he is so rich but now no one, not even him, is messing with our Jordan."

If I can help you to set up such a project, or to help one of your teachers to set up the project, please contact me.

my e-mail: e.c.bernard@comcast.net (note periods)

my website: www.ecbernard.org

Also, contact me about your building's experience so we can share it with others. Thanks for being willing to take this on.

.

CONCLUSION

In a large school, experts estimate that someone like Jordan comes along once every two to three years.

I am encouraged now that because of this peer-project, our Jordan can prosper in our building. By intervening in the cycle of bullying, our society will not be deprived of the benefits of his high intelligence and humor.

As we look at the problems we are bequeathing to the next generation to resolve, it is clear that we need intelligent people, like Jordan, who think differently. Otherwise, if mainstream thinking could resolve the problems, the problems wouldn't exist.

We need to educate non-mainstream students as much as possible so that their different perspective finds its place in our society. We cannot let passing time in school become so difficult for them that they opt out; we must speak up to keep all children emotionally safe inside our buildings.

We also need to give this text-messaging, virtual-game-playing, internet-friend-making generation the chance to showcase their goodness, and not just by volunteering to donate and collect items for unknown victims. When given a chance to volunteer, they rewarded me with a poignancy and tenderness for today's students that erased my envy for my retiring peers.

51 CONCLUSION

I frequently think about a local holocaust survivor, Gerda Weissman Klein, as she once told me that "teachers are the bridge to the future that we will never see."

And yet, our bridge builders' words will not change the bullies. Rather, we must also train the "cool" students to approach the *alpha audience* with the message that it is not cool to bully and to also offer them friendship.

Let's work together to keep that future bright for the Jordans of the world, and for all students who walk with them for four minutes a day, every day.

E.C. Bernard

52 BIBLIOGRAPHY

[1] "Barack Obama's Inaugural Address." <u>The New York Times</u> 20 January 2009. Retrieved 15 May 2009 from: http://www.nytimes.com/2009/01/20/us/politics/20text-obama.html

[2] "The Star Thrower" by Loren Eiseley. Retrieved 14 June 2009 from: http://www.rawfoodinfo.com/action/activist_starthrower.htm

ACKNOWLEDGEMENTS

I'd like to thank my school district, students, and parents for permission to share their experience in order to help others. These strong families make teaching a pleasure, and the world a better place.

A special thanks to my principal, who supports creative solutions to sticky situations.

I am profoundly grateful to the parents who told their son that all of his suffering before the project must be for some greater good; may sharing this story be that greater good. Their wisdom, patience, and extraordinary communication skills have made me a better teacher.

Eternal thanks to my husband, Ed, who doesn't complain about the countless hours alone while I write.

A heart-felt thanks to the protectors of my creativity, Jackie and my godchild, Lee. The former nudged me to address the question, "What could people tell bullies to help them stop?" The latter inspired me to move from despair to hope about sharing this story.

I am blessed with friends willing to edit my drafts on short notice. Suzanne, Linda, Donna, Paula, and Carol deserve recognition and my gratitude because they know I am lying when I say, "This will only take an hour." They read it, anyway, and still are nice to me. Thanks, girlfriends.

My sister, Anne, helps me to be a better writer and a better person. While out on our morning walks, we have

54 ACKNOWLEDGEMENTS

argued the minutia of word choice, tone and relevance. For the record, she is right only 99.8% of the time.

Although there are many fingerprints all over this story, I alone am responsible for any errors.

E.C. Bernard